The MIRACLE of Easter

MW00763277

A 4-week course to help junior higbers
understand the true meaning of Easter

Loveland, Colorado

by Steven B. Huddleston

Group®

The Miracle of Easter
Copyright © 1993 Group Publishing, Inc.

First Printing

Credits
Edited by Amy Nappa
Cover designed by Diane Whisner
Title page illustration by Dennis Auth
Illustrations by Ray Medici

Scriptures quoted from **The Youth Bible,** New Century Version, copyright © 1991 by Word Publishing, Dallas, TX 75039. Used by permission.

ISBN 1-55945-143-2
Printed in the United States of America

CONTENTS

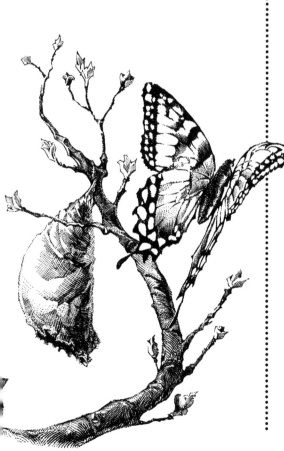

THE MIRACLE OF EASTER

"**B**races? I won't be able to smile for two years!"

Jill blushed with embarrassment when her friends teased her about her new braces. She was ashamed of her shiny smile, and the teasing of her peers brought many tears. Yet those same braces straightened her teeth and resulted in a beautiful smile, many compliments, and a healthy self-image.

A young artist didn't have time for God. He was too busy traveling the world, viewing beautiful sights, and capturing them on canvas. But one day a tragic accident blinded him, and he never painted again. Finally, in desperation, the artist turned to God and discovered the Light of the World. He later said, "It was not until my eyes were blinded that I was able to see God."

What American Teenagers Believe

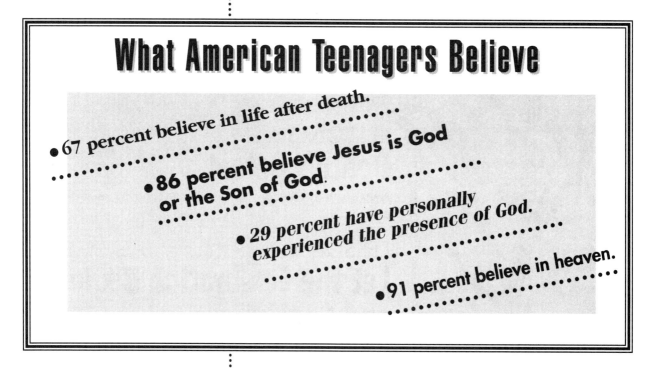

- 67 percent believe in life after death.
- 86 percent believe Jesus is God or the Son of God.
- 29 percent have personally experienced the presence of God.
- 91 percent believe in heaven.

It seems contradictory that a girl's source of humiliation could become her source of pride and that a man couldn't see until his eyes were blind, but these statements are true. They are paradoxes: true statements that seem self-contradictory.

The death and resurrection of Jesus illuminate many paradoxes. We can look forward to the future only by looking back to Calvary. The Crucifixion showed humanity at its worst, yet revealed our great worth. Death was required before new life could be obtained.

Easter should help us remember and understand this great event, but the message is often mixed. Candy, egg hunts, and the fresh creases of new Easter outfits usually receive more attention than new life in Christ.

The church can help junior high and middle school students sort through the false messages and understand the true meaning of this special season. By helping your students experience the love, victory, and hope behind Easter, you can motivate them to celebrate their new lives in Christ all year long.

By the end of this course, your students will
- understand the true meaning of Easter,
- comprehend the agony suffered by Jesus and recognize he endured this suffering because of his great love for them,
- be able to tell reasons Jesus did indeed rise from the dead, and
- find ways to express the message of Easter all year long.

COURSE OBJECTIVES

HOW TO USE THIS COURSE

Think back on an important lesson you've learned in life. Did you learn it from reading about it? from hearing about it? from something you experienced? Chances are, the most important lessons you've learned came from something you experienced. That's what active learning is— learning by doing. And active learning is a key element in Group's Active Bible Curriculum®.

Active learning leads students in doing things that help them understand important principles, messages, and ideas. It's a discovery process that helps kids internalize what they learn.

Each lesson section in Group's Active Bible Curriculum plays an important part in active learning:

The **Opener** involves kids in the topic in fun and unusual ways.

The **Action and Reflection** includes an experience designed to evoke specific feelings in the students. This section also processes those feelings through "How did you feel?" questions and applies the message to situations kids face.

The **Bible Application** actively connects the topic with the Bible. It helps kids see how the Bible is relevant to the situations they face.

The **Commitment** helps students internalize the Bible's message and commit to making changes in their lives.

The **Closing** funnels the lesson's message into a time of creative reflection and prayer.

When you put all the sections together, you get a lesson that's fun to teach. And kids get messages they'll remember.

● Read the Introduction, the Course Objectives, and This Course at a Glance.

● Decide how you'll publicize the course using the clip art on the Publicity Page (p. 9). Prepare fliers, newsletter articles, and posters as needed.

● Look at the Bonus Ideas (p. 43) and decide which ones you'll use.

● Read the opening statements, Objectives, and Bible Basis for the lesson. The Bible Basis shows how specific passages relate to junior highers and middle schoolers today.

● Choose which Opener and Closing options to use. Each is appropriate for a different kind of group.

● Gather necessary supplies from This Lesson at a Glance.

● Read each section of the lesson. Adjust where necessary for your class size and meeting room.

● The approximate minutes listed give you an idea of how long each activity will take. Each lesson is designed to take 35 to 60 minutes. Shorten or lengthen activities as needed to fit your group.

● If you see you're going to have extra time, do an activity or two from the "If You Still Have Time . . . " box or from the Bonus Ideas (p. 43).

● Dive into the activities with the kids. Don't be a spectator. The lesson will be more successful and rewarding to both you and your students.

● Though some kids may at first think certain activities are "silly," they'll enjoy them and they'll remember the messages from these activities long after the lesson is over. As one Active Bible Curriculum user has said, "I can ask the kids questions about a lesson I did three weeks ago, and they actually remember what I taught!" And that's the whole idea of teaching . . . isn't it?

● The answers given after discussion questions are responses your students *might* give. They aren't the only answers or the "right" answers. If needed, use them to spark discussion. Kids won't always say what you wish they'd say. That's why some of the responses given are negative or controversial. If someone responds negatively, don't be shocked. Accept the person and use the opportunity to explore other angles of the issue.

Have fun with the activities you lead. Remember, it is Jesus who encourages us to become "like little children." Besides, how often do your kids get *permission* to express their childlike qualities?

THIS COURSE AT A GLANCE

Before you dive into the lessons, familiarize yourself with each lesson aim. Then read the Scripture passages.
- Study them as a background to the lessons.
- Use them as a basis for your personal devotions.
- Think about how they relate to kids' circumstances today.

LESSON 1: BYE-BYE, BUNNY

Lesson Aim: To help junior highers focus on the real meaning of Easter.

Bible Basis: Exodus 12:1-14; Mark 14:12, 22-25.

LESSON 2: AT THE CROSS

Lesson Aim: To help students recognize the depth of God's love for them by understanding the pain and the purpose of the Crucifixion.

Bible Basis: Mark 15:16-37.

LESSON 3: DEATH'S DEFEAT

Lesson Aim: To help students discover Jesus Christ's power over death and sin.

Bible Basis: Matthew 28:1-15.

LESSON 4: LET THE CELEBRATION BEGIN, AND CONTINUE!

Lesson Aim: To help students recognize and celebrate the hope of eternal life we have because of the Resurrection.

Bible Basis: 1 Corinthians 15:17-22, 42-44.

PUBLICITY PAGE

Grab your junior highers' attention! Photocopy this page, and then cut and paste the art of your choice in your church bulletin or newsletter to advertise this course on Easter. Or photocopy and use the ready-made flier as a bulletin insert. Permission to photocopy this clip art is **granted for local** church use.

Splash this clip art on posters, **fliers, or even** postcards! Just add the vital **details: the date and** time the course begins and whe**re you'll meet.**

It's that simple.

The Miracle of Easter

A 4-week course to help junior highers and middle school students understand the true meaning of Easter

Come to _____

On _____

At _____

Come learn what really happened on the first Easter and how it can change your life forever!

BYE-BYE, BUNNY

During Easter most kids are so busy coloring eggs and eating candy that they barely give a thought to the death and resurrection of Jesus Christ.

Examining what's behind Easter traditions can help students better understand and celebrate the true meaning of this special holiday.

To help junior highers focus on the real meaning of Easter.

LESSON AIM

Students will
- **explore misleading messages about Easter,**
- **see how Easter myths lead people away from the holiday's true meaning, and**
- **discover how Jesus gave new meaning to an old religious celebration.**

OBJECTIVES

Look up the following Scriptures. Then read the background paragraphs to see how the passages relate to your junior highers and middle schoolers.

BIBLE BASIS
EXODUS 12:1-14
MARK 14:12, 22-25

Exodus 12:1-14 records God's directions for the first Passover meal. The Israelites were told what to prepare and when and how to eat it. Death would pass over the homes of those who marked their door frames with the blood of the lamb as God had instructed.

This passage explains the background of a continuing tradition. Students will see how the Passover celebration originated and understand its importance.

In **Mark 14:12, 22-25** Jesus celebrated Passover with his disciples. During this meal Jesus revealed a new and deeper meaning for this celebration. Just as the Israelites were saved by the blood of the lamb many years before, salvation would now be provided by the blood of Jesus himself, the Lamb of God.

Jesus took an ancient holiday ritual and gave it new

meaning through his death on the cross. This passage can help junior highers see past the rabbits, eggs, and candy of the Easter tradition and begin to recognize a deeper meaning behind the symbols of Easter.

THIS LESSON AT A GLANCE

Section	Minutes	What Students Will Do	Supplies
Opener (Option 1)	5 to 10	**Zippin' and Rippin'**—Find pictures illustrating words associated with Easter.	Old magazines
(Option 2)		**Traditions**—Share family traditions and their origins.	
Action and Reflection	10 to 15	**What's the Meaning of This?**—Pantomime messages.	
Bible Application	10 to 15	**What's New?**—Discover how Jesus gave an old religious celebration new meaning.	Tablecloth, unleavened bread, cup, fruit juice, Bible
Commitment	10 to 15	**Eggstra-Special Basket**—Share ways others have added life to the group.	"Basket and Eggs" handouts (p. 18), scissors, stapler, pencils
Closing (Option 1)	up to 5	**Bean Thankful**—Thank God for new changes in life.	Bowl, jelly beans
(Option 2)		**Ritual Reminder**—Develop new family rituals in observance of Easter.	

The Lesson

OPENER
(5 to 10 minutes)

☐ OPTION 1: ZIPPIN' AND RIPPIN'

Form teams of no more than four. Give each team an old magazine.

Say: **I'm looking for pictures to illustrate various words. When I read a word from my list, your team has 20 seconds to zip through your magazine and find a picture representing that word. Rip the picture out and bring it to me. When time is up, I'll choose the picture that best depicts the word I've read. The team with the most accurate pictures wins.**

To help the teams work more efficiently, have kids tear the magazines into sections. Each team member can look through his or her section to find an appropriate picture for the team.

Read the following words, allowing 20 seconds after each word for teams to complete their searches:

Love

Hope

Death
Victory
Easter

Congratulate the winning team and ask:
● **How difficult was it for your team to decide on a picture?** (It was easy because there were obvious pictures; it was hard because we had a lot of good options to choose from.)
● **What were you looking for when I said "Easter"?** (A rabbit; eggs; a cross; flowers.)
● **Why do you think these images best represent this holiday?** (Because we get candy then; because it's spring; because Jesus rose from the dead then.)
● **How do the other words I read relate to Easter?** (Jesus died because he loved us; Easter celebrates Christ's victory over death.)

Say: **Over the years people have thought of many things when they heard the word "Easter." The true meaning of this holiday often gets lost behind traditions and decorations. Today we're going to see how various traditions were started and find how they can bring us closer to the real meaning of Easter.**

Teacher Tip

If you don't have a watch with a second hand, slowly count to 20 to measure 20 seconds.

☐ OPTION 2: TRADITIONS

Have students form groups of no more than four.

Say: **Share with your group a tradition your family has and how it began (if you know). Perhaps you have a funny crown that's worn during birthday dinners, or you always go out for fast food on Sunday.**

After group members have shared, ask:
● **What traditions seemed funny or unusual to you?** (Answers will vary.)
● **What holiday traditions or customs are so popular it seems everyone observes them?** (Lighting and blowing out birthday candles; giving a tie to Dad on Father's Day; putting hearts on everything during February.)
● **What traditions and customs do people associate with Easter?** (Coloring and hunting for eggs; getting new clothes; getting a basket full of candy.)
● **Do you think these traditions represent the true meaning of Easter? Explain.** (Yes, new things represent new life; no, Easter is about Jesus coming back to life; I'm not sure what Easter really means.)

Say: **Today we're going to look at Easter traditions and customs to see what they have to do with the actual holiday. We'll also find ways these customs help us understand the true meaning of Easter.**

WHAT'S THE MEANING OF THIS?

Have students form three groups. Secretly assign each group one of the following actions to pantomime to the other groups: riding a blue motorcycle, washing an elephant, and water-skiing behind a rowboat. Explain that no sounds of any kind will be allowed, and the other groups must guess the *exact* thing being acting out.

Give each group one minute to pantomime its action. If the other groups are unable to guess correctly within this time, allow students to tell what they were pantomiming, then have the next group perform.

When all groups are finished, ask:

● **What were you thinking while you were acting out one thing and everyone was interpreting it to mean something else?** (I was frustrated; I was thinking I must look like a fool!)

● **How did it feel when someone finally understood the meaning behind your actions?** (Good; I was relieved; I felt like we'd done a good job.)

● **What was the overall reaction when someone correctly guessed what another was doing?** (Everyone seemed relieved; we were excited to be right; the people who were acting seemed happy to be done!)

● **What message do you think God gives us about Easter?** (It's about new life; Easter is when Christ rose from the dead; I don't know.)

● **How is God giving us this message like when you were trying to explain something to the other groups?** (We've mixed up the message; God must be frustrated; God probably feels happy when we understand what the real message is.)

● **How have we mixed up Christ's Easter message?** (By saying Easter is about eggs and new clothes; by only thinking of Easter as a time we get out of school.)

● **How can associating Easter with egg hunts and candy keep people from knowing the truth?** (They may never think to look for the true meaning of the holiday; they may think Easter is only a fun holiday and not about Christ; it could be like Christmas since people think that's only about Santa and not Jesus' birth.)

Say: **Jesus wanted to be sure that we'd understand the true message of what he did for us on the cross. So Jesus took an old Jewish tradition and gave it new meaning to illustrate what his death and resurrection meant.**

WHAT'S NEW?

Spread a tablecloth on the floor and place a single piece of unleavened bread (pita bread works nicely) and a cup of fruit juice on it.

Have students recline on the floor around the cloth. Choose a student to read Exodus 12:1-14 aloud. If you have more than 10 students in your class, form two or three groups and have each group form a circle around unleavened bread and fruit juice.

Ask:

● **What was the significance of this meal?** (God was about to rescue the Israelites from the Egyptians.)

● **The people had to be ready to leave immediately. How do God's instructions focus on this?** (The bread was baked without allowing time for it to rise; they wore traveling clothes while eating; they had to eat fast.)

● **What did God want the Israelites to remember when they celebrated this meal each year?** (How God saved them from death; God saves faithful followers; God has power over life and death.)

Say: **This feast of celebration is known as Passover because death passed over those who followed God. The Bible tells of Jesus and his disciples celebrating the Passover meal in Mark 14:12, 22-25.**

Have another student read these verses.

Ask:

● **What new meaning for this meal did Jesus explain to his followers?** (The bread was to remind them of his broken body; the cup of wine was to remind them of his blood.)

● **How did Jesus' death on the cross give new meaning to Passover?** (He represents the lamb that was sacrificed; his blood saves us from spiritual death.)

● **What new meanings could we give to some of the things we commonly associate with Easter, such as rabbits or eggs?** (Eggs could represent new life; since rabbits hop around a lot they could represent joy.)

Say: **We can give new meanings to old traditions, but it's important for us to remember that the true meaning of Easter came from God. When Christ died and rose again we received the opportunity for new spiritual life.**

Note: If Communion in this setting is permitted by your church doctrines, partake of the bread and cup together.

EGGSTRA-SPECIAL BASKET

Photocopy the "Basket and Eggs" handout (p. 18), allowing one for each student. (You may prepare extra "eggs" and have students use more in this activity if you like.) Have kids cut out and staple the baskets according to the handout directions. Have them each write their names on their baskets and on one side of each of their four eggs. Gather the eggs, mix them, and redistribute them so each student has four eggs with the names of various students on them.

Say: **On the blank side of each egg write one way the person whose name is on the other side adds life to our group. For example, you could write, "You laughter adds life to our group," or "Your enthusiasm adds life to our group."**

COMMITMENT
(10 to 15 minutes)

When everyone has completed this, have students return the eggs to their owners' baskets.

Ask:

● **How has Christ given new life to our group?** (By giving us eternal life; by giving us a reason to be happy; by helping us with our problems.)

● **How can we express our appreciation for this new life?** (By telling others; by remembering to thank God; by showing we have new life through our actions.)

Say: **Each of you adds something special to our group, but what Christ has added is truly life-changing. Let's remember the true meaning of Easter this year by expressing our appreciation in the ways you've named.**

Table Talk

The "Table Talk" activity in this course helps junior highers and middle schoolers discuss with their parents the true meaning of Easter.

If you choose to use the "Table Talk" activity, this is a good time to show students the "Table Talk" handout (p. 19.) Ask them to spend time with their parents completing it.

Before kids leave, give them each the "Table Talk" handout to take home, or tell them you'll be sending it to their parents. Tell kids to be prepared to report next week on their experiences with the handout.

Or use the "Table Talk" idea found in the Bonus Ideas (p. 44) for a meeting based on the handout.

CLOSING
(up to 5 minutes)

☐ OPTION 1: BEAN THANKFUL

Pass a large bowl of jelly beans around and allow students to take as many as they want, but don't let them eat any. Have kids form groups of no more than four.

Say: **For each jelly bean you took, express thanks for a way God has brought newness to your life through Christ. Perhaps God has helped you get along better with your family or given you a new attitude about school. After each thing you thank God for, eat one of your jelly beans. We'll continue until everyone's eaten all their jelly beans.**

Tell kids it's OK if they repeat what others say.

☐ OPTION 2: RITUAL REMINDER

Form groups of no more than four and have each group come up with several new rituals their families could add to their Easter celebrations. For example, a family could place a big rock by the door of their home to remind them of the stone rolled away from the tomb. Then have each group share its best idea with the rest of the class.

Say: **No matter what you use as a reminder, let's always**

remember the importance of Easter.

Close with prayer, thanking Christ for bringing new life and new meaning to an old tradition.

If You Still Have Time . . .

Write-a-Rhyme—Have each student write a poem expressing the true meaning of Easter. Invite students to share their poems with the class, then display the poems in the church foyer or other locations where the congregation will be able to see them.

Easter . . . NOT!—If you used the "Zippin' and Rippin'" opener, have kids look through what's left of the magazines and cut out pictures that misrepresent Easter. (If you didn't use this opener, have students draw pictures misrepresenting Easter.)

Have students make a collage with the heading, "Easter . . . NOT!" Display the poster in the classroom as a reminder of the true meaning of this holiday.

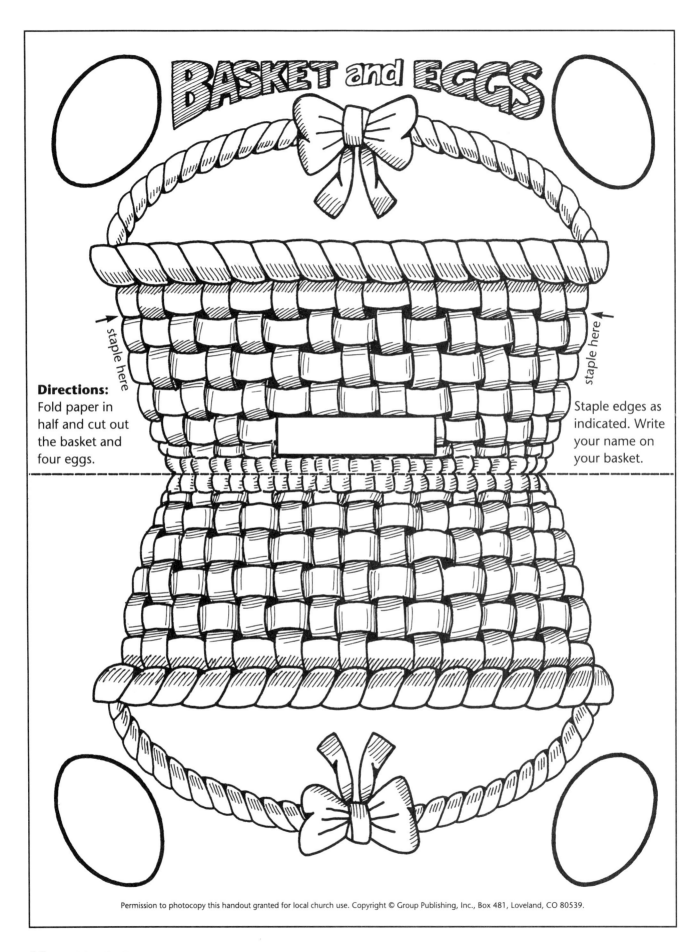

BASKET and EGGS

Directions:
Fold paper in half and cut out the basket and four eggs.

staple here

staple here

Staple edges as indicated. Write your name on your basket.

Table Talk

To the Parent: We're involved in a junior high course at church called *The Miracle of Easter.* Students are exploring the true meaning of this holiday and how it can make a difference in their lives. We'd like you and your teenager to discuss this important topic. Use this "Table Talk" page to help you do that.

Parent

Complete the following sentences:
- When I was your age, the thing I liked most about Easter was...
- The biggest sacrifice of love I ever made was...
- A time when Christ helped me be victorious over a difficult situation was...
- One thing I do to keep my hope in Christ alive is...

Junior higher

Complete the following sentences:
- Something I look forward to each Easter is...
- If I were present when Jesus was crucified, I think I would have...
- One struggle I need to gain victory over is...
- The thing about heaven I look forward to the most is...

Parent and junior higher

Read 1 Peter 1:3-9 together and discuss how the resurrection of Jesus can give you joy even in suffering. What is one new tradition your family could establish to help celebrate the true meaning of Easter?

The MIRACLE of Easter

LESSON 2

AT THE CROSS

Young people want desperately to be loved. They may see themselves as unworthy of love or look to others to find self-worth. This lesson encourages students by helping them see how valuable they are to God.

LESSON AIM

To help students recognize the depth of God's love for them by understanding the pain and the purpose of the Crucifixion.

OBJECTIVES

Students will
- witness the suffering of an innocent person,
- recognize the pain and sacrifice involved in the Crucifixion, and
- ask God for forgiveness by nailing their sins to a cross.

BLE BASIS

MARK 15:16-37

Look up the following verses. Then read the background paragraphs to see how the passage relates to your junior highers and middle schoolers.

Mark 15:16-37 tells of Jesus' crucifixion and death. This passage details the cruel ways Jesus was tortured before his painful death on the cross. It also reveals the way Christ was mocked and ridiculed by the very people for whom he was dying.

This passage shows students the incredible suffering Jesus endured out of love for them. At a time when junior highers may feel uncertain about their "loveliness," this account of Christ's death will reassure them of how truly valuable they are. An innocent man was willing to be punished and die in their place.

Section	Minutes	What Students Will Do	Supplies
Opener (Option 1)	5 to 10	**Would I Die for You?**—Consider who they'd die for and how much love it would require.	Tape, newsprint, pencils, Bible
(Option 2)		**It's a Different World**—Evaluate how past events have changed the course of history.	
Action and Reflection	10 to 15	**Sundae Suffering**—Observe an innocent person being unjustly punished.	Bibles, dropcloth, ice cream, toppings, towels
Bible Application	15 to 20	**Crucifixion Quiz**—Discover the extreme suffering Jesus endured on the cross.	Bibles, 3/8×10-inch nail, hammer, pencils, "Crucifixion Quiz" handouts (p. 27)
Commitment	5 to 10	**Nail It to the Cross**—Experience forgiveness of sins by "nailing" them to a cross.	Wooden cross, nails, black construction paper, hammer, Bible
Closing (Option 1)	up to 5	**Sack-rifice**—Name ways to show love to God in the coming week.	Lunch sacks, pencils, 3×5 cards
(Option 2)		**Thankful Heart**—Identify ways God's love has changed their lives.	Red construction paper, scissors, pencils, tape, cross from "Nail It to the Cross" activity

The Lesson

☐ OPTION 1: WOULD I DIE FOR YOU?

Tape a sheet of newsprint with the heading, "I'd Die For..." on the wall. As students enter the room, have them list all the people or things they'd be willing to die for. Remind kids to think seriously before listing anyone or anything on the newsprint.

Ask:

● **Why would you be willing to die for these?** (Answers will vary.)

Say: **If there's anything or anyone on this list you dislike, come up and circle that item or name.**

Allow students to do this.

Say: **If you feel you'd truly be willing to give up everything and suffer death for the people or things you listed, then fall to the floor in a mock death scene.**

After students have fallen, read Romans 5:7 aloud.

Say: **These people and things must be special to you if**

OPENER
(5 to 10 minutes)

you'd actually die for them. But Jesus' love is so great, he actually chose to die for not only his friends but also for his enemies. Today we'll see how God showed love for us through Jesus' death on the cross.

☐ OPTION 2: IT'S A DIFFERENT WORLD

Form four groups. (A group can be one person if necessary.) Ask each group one of the questions below and have kids think of as many answers as possible.

Group 1: **How would our lives be different if aspirin had never been invented?**

Group 2: **How would our lives be different if Hitler had won World War II?**

Group 3: **How would our lives be different if slavery hadn't been abolished?**

Group 4: **How would our lives be different if electricity hadn't been invented?**

After a few moments have each group share its question and answers with the rest of the class.

Say: **Different events in history have profoundly changed our lives. But nothing has had a greater impact on us than Jesus' death and resurrection. Today we'll be looking at this historical event and how it shows God's great love for us.**

Table Talk Follow-Up

If you sent the "Table Talk" handout (p. 19) to parents last week, discuss students' reactions to the activity. Ask volunteers to share what they learned from the discussion with their parents.

ACTION AND REFLECTION
(10 to 15 minutes)

SUNDAE SUFFERING

Form two teams and name one person to represent each team in a Bible quiz.

Say: **The job of each team is to cheer its representative on to victory. You may coach your representative if you think you know the right answer, but only the representative may tell me the answer.**

Do *not* explain the punishment before a team selects a representative, and don't let anyone switch places with a representative at this point.

Say: **Because the whole team is counting on him (or her), the losing representative will be "punished" by being turned into a human ice cream sundae.**

Play the game by asking the following questions about Easter. The first person to answer correctly gets 1 point, and the first person with 3 points wins. If students seem to be having trouble answering the questions, team members may look for answers in their Bibles during the quiz.

Ask:

● **What did the soldiers use to make a crown for Jesus?** (Thorny branches.)

● **What's one of the ways the soldiers tortured Jesus before killing him?** (Beating him with sticks; whipping him; spitting on him.)

● **What was the name of the governor who allowed Jesus to be killed?** (Pilate.)

● **How many robbers were crucified alongside Jesus?** (Two.)

● **What was the name of the man who buried Jesus?** (Joseph of Arimathea.)

● **Who was the first person to see Jesus after he rose from the dead?** (Mary Magdalene.)

After you have declared a winner, have the losing representative prepare for "punishment." Have him or her sit on a folding chair with a sheet of plastic underneath to protect the floor. Bring out ice cream and toppings such as chocolate syrup, whipped cream, and, of course, a cherry. Laugh and joke about what a mess you're going to make of this person's hair and clothes.

Just before making the "sundae," have another leader or student who's agreed ahead of time come forward and volunteer to take the punishment for the losing representative. Have them trade places, then proceed to make the ice cream sundae on the volunteer's head. The volunteer will obviously be uncomfortable, but it will not hurt him or her.

When you're finished, have everyone cheer for the volunteer, then send him or her out to clean up. (Have plenty of towels handy.)

Ask the losing representative:

● **How did it make you feel to let someone else suffer in your place?** (I was relieved; I felt guilty; thankful.)

Ask the class:

● **What were you thinking as you watched an innocent person suffer?** (I felt sorry; I'm glad it wasn't me; I didn't think it was fair.)

● **How was this activity like what Jesus did on the cross?** (He chose to take our punishment for us; he suffered so we wouldn't have to.)

● **Why did Jesus have to die?** (So we wouldn't have to suffer; so we could have a relationship with God; so we could go to heaven.)

● **How does it make you feel to know that Jesus took your place on the cross?** (Relieved; guilty; thankful.)

● **How do you think the people closest to Jesus must have felt as they watched him suffer and die?** (Sorry; confused; they didn't think it was fair; sad.)

Read John 3:16.

Say: **We can see from this exercise how fortunate we are that Christ took our punishment for us. But we can't truly appreciate the depth of his love until we can better understand just how much he suffered for us.**

CRUCIFIXION QUIZ

Have students open their Bibles to Mark 15:16-37.

Say: **As I read this passage aloud, follow along in your Bibles. Each time I come to a place where a group of people, such as soldiers, are speaking, I'll stop. At that point everyone should read aloud what the people were saying. Say the words with feeling, as if you were really there.**

(Don't worry if students read from various versions of the Bible. This will give the reading more of a "crowd" effect with everyone calling out at once.)

Read the passage aloud, stopping during verses 18, 29-30, 31-32, and 35-36 for students to speak. As you read, pass a ⅜×10-inch nail around the room to give students an idea of what went into Christ's hands and feet. (These nails can be purchased in hardware stores for about 50 cents apiece.) Also, have another leader in the back of the room pound a hammer every three or four seconds.

After reading the Scripture, give each student a pencil and a photocopy of the "Crucifixion Quiz" handout (p. 27). Have kids form groups of no more than four and work together on the quiz. After several minutes regroup to go over the answers. Before explaining the correct responses, have groups explain their answers. Use the key below to fill in information kids may be unaware of.

Answers to "Crucifixion Quiz"

1. FALSE. Jesus was whipped with a cat-o'-nine-tails. This whip had nine straps, and each strap usually had a piece of glass, metal, or a sharp stone at the tip which was dragged across the victim's back with each lash.

2. FALSE. Crosses were close enough to the ground to allow spectators to hit the victims, poke them with sticks, or spit on them.

3. TRUE. The nails probably went between the two bones in his wrists and into the feet right above the heels.

4. FALSE. Most likely, he suffocated. As the cross was lifted vertically and dropped into its stand, it was common for the victim's arms to pop out of their sockets. The rib cage then pressed against the lungs, making breathing almost impossible. Victims would have to pull themselves up on their displaced arms and pierced hands just to take a breath or speak, then they would collapse once again.

5. TRUE. This was to further humiliate the victim. Soldiers gambled for Jesus' clothes at the foot of the cross.

6. FALSE. The Bible makes it clear that although Jesus

was God, he was also fully human. He got hungry, thirsty, and tired. He felt the pain of the cross the same way you or I would.

7. TRUE. He had to endure the cruelty and mocking of the very people he was dying for. His closest friends had abandoned him. And worst of all, for that brief moment in history when he took our sins upon himself, even God turned away.

Ask:

● **How has this reading and quiz made you feel about Jesus' death?** (Sad; sick because of the way he was treated; grossed out.)

● **Why do you think Jesus was willing to endure this?** (Because he loved us; because he knew what the outcome would be; he knew he'd come back to life.)

● **If you had to die in the same fashion as Jesus, is there anyone or anything you would still die for? Why or why not?** (Yes, I love someone that much; no, I don't think I could go through that for anyone.)

● **How does knowing what Jesus went through for you make you feel about him?** (It makes me have more respect for him; it makes me more thankful; I feel really loved by God.)

Say: **Knowing what Christ went through can help us understand the depth of his love for us. Any innocent person who would go through this torture must have incredible love for others.**

NAIL IT TO THE CROSS

Place a wooden cross at one end of the room. Give students each a strip of black construction paper and a nail.

Say: **This paper represents your sins. Think of specific things you've done wrong for which you'd like to be forgiven.**

Give students a moment for quiet reflection.

Say: **Our sins made it necessary for Jesus to be nailed to the cross. If we had never sinned, Jesus wouldn't have had to suffer. The cross represents God's great love for us and willingness to forgive all our sins.**

Have students take their "sins" and actually nail them to the cross. (If you are using a cardboard cross, have them tape their sins to the cross.) As they're placing their sins on the cross, have kids silently ask God to forgive their sins.

Read Romans 5:6-9.

Say: **Jesus could have refused to die, but he chose to endure suffering and death because of his deep love for you and me. Now we have the opportunity to respond to this love.**

COMMITMENT
(5 to 10 minutes)

TEACHER TIP

A life-size wooden cross can be made by nailing together two 2×4-inch pieces of lumber—one 8 feet and the other 4 feet in length. This can be propped against a wall in the classroom. A cross could also be made of cardboard or poster board if necessary.

CLOSING

☐ OPTION 1: SACK-RIFICE

Give each student a paper lunch sack, a pencil, and seven 3×5 cards. Have them each draw a cross on their sack.

Say: **On each card write one thing you can do this week to show your love to God for his great sacrifice. For example, "Write a letter of thanks to God," or "Tell everyone in my family I love them because God loves me." When you've written something different on each card, put them all in your sack.**

Allow several moments for students to complete this. If students are unable to think of seven things have them ask others for suggestions.

Say: **Take this sack home and pull out one card each day this week. Do what you've written as a way to express your love to God.**

☐ OPTION 2: THANKFUL HEART

Give each student a sheet of red construction paper, scissors, and a pencil. Have kids each cut out a heart shape and write on it different ways God's love has changed their lives. For example, "God's love has made me more patient," or "God's love has helped me be kind to people I don't really like."

Have students take turns taping their paper hearts over the black "sins" on the cross used in the "Nail It to the Cross" activity. As kids place their hearts on the cross have them pray, "Thank you, God, for..." and then say what they wrote on their hearts.

If You Still Have Time . . .

The Drawbridge—Tell the story of the man who operated a drawbridge for the railroad. (This story is available on the cassette tape *Instant Devotions for Youth Ministry* through Group Publishing.)

A drawbridge operator took his small son to work with him. When it was time to lower the bridge, the boy was missing. After frantically searching, the man saw his son caught under the drawbridge. If he pulled the lever to lower the bridge, his son would be crushed to death by the gears. But if he ran out and saved his son, there would be no time to lower the bridge before the train crossed and all on board would be killed.

Have the students discuss what they would do if they were the father, and how this story is like what God did for us.

Pass-a-Cross—Have the class form a large circle. Carry the cross used in the "Nail It to the Cross" activity to one of the kids. Share a positive trait that person has and tell him or her that Jesus died so he or she could use that trait for him. For instance, "Tom, you have a great sense of humor, and Jesus died on the cross so you could use that sense of humor to serve him." Give the cross to the person you shared with and have him or her carry the cross to someone else in the circle and share a positive trait in the same manner. Have the kids continue to pass the cross until all students have received and passed the cross.

CRUCIFIXION QUIZ

Discuss these questions in your groups and answer either true or false to each one.

_____1. When Jesus was whipped 39 lashes, the whip used was much like the bullwhips we see today.

_____2. The cross hung high over everyone's head.

_____3. Nails were driven through Jesus' hands or wrists and feet, and when the cross was lifted, all his weight rested on these nail-pierced wounds.

_____4. Jesus probably bled to death.

_____5. Jesus was probably naked, or at least nearly naked, as he hung on the cross.

_____6. Since Jesus was the Son of God, he didn't feel pain the same way we would.

_____7. The greatest pain Jesus suffered on the cross probably wasn't physical pain, but emotional pain.

LESSON 3

DEATH'S DEFEAT

As kids enter their teenage years they discover that "hand-me-down religion" and blind faith aren't sufficient to deal with the doubts and dilemmas they're facing. Closer examination and acceptance of Christ's resurrection can help students make intelligent decisions about their faith.

LESSON AIM

To help students discover Jesus Christ's power over death and sin.

OBJECTIVES

Students will
- recognize that faith is required for both belief and unbelief,
- determine ways to come to believe in something,
- examine evidence for the Resurrection, and
- discover how the truth of the Resurrection brings them victory over sin.

BIBLE BASIS
MATTHEW 28:1-15

Look up the following verses. Then read the background paragraphs to see how the passage relates to your junior highers and middle schoolers.

Matthew 28:1-15 records Jesus' resurrection from the dead. This passage tells how the stone was rolled from the tomb and how an angel spoke to the women looking for Jesus. Then Jesus met the women and his followers. As they were worshiping him, others were devising false explanations for the empty tomb.

Jesus' resurrection is vital to the Christian faith. If Jesus had no power over death, we would have no hope of eternal life. Junior highers can learn the importance of believing in a risen Savior and understand the power they have over sin as a result of this Resurrection.

Section	Minutes	What Students Will Do	Supplies
Opener (Option 1)	5 to 10	**The Chicken, the Fox, and the Feed**—Compare a puzzle to beliefs about the Resurrection.	
(Option 2)		**Is It There?**—Discover the difference between blind faith and intelligent faith.	Silver dollar or other coin, Bible
Action and Reflection	10 to 15	**Deduction Junction**—Find the correct card out of many.	3×5 cards
Bible Application	15 to 20	**Body Search**—Evaluate various empty-tomb theories.	"Body Search" handout (p. 36), scissors, pencils, Bibles
Commitment	5 to 10	**Victory Pennants**—Receive encouragement to live victoriously for Jesus.	Bible, markers, construction paper, scissors, tape
Closing (Option 1)	up to 5	**Musical Easter Basket**—Share Easter thoughts and experiences.	Scissors, pen, 3×5 cards, basket, tape player, music tape
(Option 2)		**Because He Lives**—Reflect on the blessings and responsibilities we have because of the Resurrection.	Old bedsheet, markers, large ball

The Lesson

☐ OPTION 1: THE CHICKEN, THE FOX, AND THE FEED

Share the following puzzle with the class:

There was a farmer who lived on an island. He rowed his boat to the mainland one day and bought a fox, a chicken, and a bag of chicken feed. His boat would only hold himself and one other item at a time, so he'd have to make more than one trip to get everything home. He couldn't leave the fox and chicken on land together because the fox would eat the chicken. He couldn't leave the chicken and feed together because the chicken would eat the feed. Is it possible for the farmer to take all three items back to his island without ever leaving the chicken with the seed or the fox?

Give students a few seconds to think about this puzzle. Then have all who believe it's possible stand on one side of the room. Have all who think it's not possible stand on the other side of the room.

Ask:

● **Why do those who think it's *possible* believe so?** (I

OPENER
(5 to 10 minutes)

know how he could do it; I don't know how, but I still believe there's a way; I just went where everyone else was going.)

● **Why do those who think it's *impossible* believe so?** (I don't see any way to do it, so I don't think he could; I just went where everyone was going.)

● **Can anyone prove you've come to the right conclusion?**

See if anyone has solved the puzzle. If not, explain the solution: **Yes, the farmer can do it. He'd take the chicken to the island first, then come back for the fox. When he dropped the fox off at the island, he would put the chicken back in the boat and return to the mainland. He'd then leave the chicken on the mainland while he took the feed to the island. Finally, he would bring the chicken back to the island.**

Ask:

● **How's the choice you made like the way some people choose what they believe about Jesus coming back to life after being killed?** (They form beliefs without any real proof to support them; they think it through before making a decision; they just believe what other people around them believe.)

Say: **When it comes to believing in Jesus' resurrection, we don't need to rely on hunches or opinions. Today we'll be looking at evidence giving us sure knowledge that Jesus is risen.**

☐ OPTION 2: IS IT THERE?

Hold up a silver dollar (or other coin) for all to see.
Ask:

● **Who believes I'm holding a silver dollar? Does it take faith for you to believe that?** (No, because we can see it.)

Have someone read Hebrews 11:1. Then put the coin in your pocket and pull your hand back out with your fist clenched so kids cannot see if the silver dollar is in your hand or not.
Ask:

● **Now how many believe there's a silver dollar in my hand? Does it take faith for you to believe that?** (Yes, because we can't see it.)

● **Is it blind faith or intelligent faith? Explain.** (Blind, because there's no evidence that the coin is in your hand instead of your pocket.)

Open your hand and show that the silver dollar is not there. Then reach into your pocket one more time and pull your hand out with your fist clenched around the coin.

Say: **The coin's in my hand. I'm not a liar, and I'm not kidding, so you can believe me.**

Ask:

● **How many believe the coin's in my hand? Is it a blind faith or an intelligent faith? Explain.** (Intelligent, because we have your word as evidence; blind, because I still don't trust you.)

Call one student up to peek into your hand and have him or her tell the class if the coin is there. Ask one more time if they have a blind faith or an intelligent faith, then open your hand to reveal the coin.

Ask:

● **Does it take faith to believe Jesus rose from the dead?** (Yes, we can't see him; yes, we can't prove his resurrection scientifically.)

● **Does it take faith to not believe Jesus rose from the dead?** (Yes, because we can't prove that he *doesn't* exist either; no, because I think coming back to life is impossible, no matter what.)

Say: **Many people have drawn conclusions about Jesus' resurrection with nothing more than blind faith. But this isn't necessary. There's plenty of evidence to help us make an intelligent decision.**

DEDUCTION JUNCTION

For this activity you'll need 10 3×5 cards for each team. Number each set of cards one through 10 on one side only.

Form teams of no more than six. Have students number themselves one to six. (If a team has less than six members, some kids will need to take two numbers.) Across from each team place a set of cards face down on the floor.

Say: **The object of this game is for each team member to find the card with his or her number on it. For example, if your number is two, you'll need to find the card with a two on it. When it's your turn, run to the set of cards and select one by turning it over. If it's the correct number, quickly mix the cards and again lay them face down before returning to your team. If it's not the correct number, do 10 jumping jacks and then turn another card over. You'll need to keep selecting cards and doing 10 jumping jacks after each incorrect card until you find the right one. Then mix the cards and turn them face down for the next person. The first team to have all members find their correct cards wins.**

Begin the activity. Monitor students as they turn over cards to be sure no one cheats. Also be sure the person mixing the cards doesn't try to place them in a specific order for the next team member.

Congratulate the team that finishes first and have all students sit down.

Ask:

● **How did you feel trying to pick the right card on the first try?** (I felt hopeless because there was no way to know which one it was; I felt lucky because I guessed right.)

● **What were you thinking as more cards in your set were eliminated?** (I was still frustrated; I was more confident because my odds of finding the right card were increasing.)

● **Why were you more likely to find the right card after**

several tries? (The odds were more in my favor; even if I didn't know which card to pick, I at least knew which cards not to pick.)

● **How was this game like or unlike the way we determine our beliefs concerning Jesus' resurrection?** (The more we know, the more wrong answers we can eliminate; the more we know about what not to believe, the more confident we can be that our faith's correct.)

Say: **Just as there were many different cards for you to choose from, there are many different theories about what actually happened after Jesus died. Let's look at them and, as in this game, find the right answer by getting rid of the wrong answers.**

BODY SEARCH

Before the meeting, photocopy and cut apart the "Body Search" handout (p. 36) as directed.

Form four groups. Give each group one section of the handout and a pencil.

Have each group determine which member will be the informant (reading to the group), the pen pusher (taking notes on the discussion), and the agent (speaking for the group during questioning). All other members will be promoters (making sure each person participates).

(If groups have less than four members, have students take more than one role.)

Say: **I've given you some of the most common theories about what happened after Jesus died. Together read the theory I've given you and list reasons why this theory could be true or why it could be false.**

After a couple minutes have groups read Matthew 28:1-15 together.

Say: **Continue your discussion, taking into account this new information.**

Allow several minutes for discussion, then have the agent for the swoon theory share his or her group's theory and conclusions.

Ask the following questions to all students, regardless of which theory they discussed:

● **Thinking back to our last lesson, what happened to Jesus before he was hung on the cross?** (He was beaten; he was whipped.)

● **If Jesus hadn't died, what might his condition have been like after this treatment?** (He'd be half-dead; he'd be weak; he'd be helpless.)

● **Could a person in this condition roll a huge and heavy stone away from the tomb's opening?** (No, it wouldn't be possible; he'd be too weak.)

Say: **Another problem with this theory is that John 19:34 says a soldier thrust a spear into Jesus' side to be sure he was dead. Blood and water came out of this**

Teacher Tip

If groups have more than six members, form eight or more groups. Photocopy the handout as needed, ensuring each theory is represented at least once.

wound, showing that Jesus had been dead long enough for his bodily fluids to separate from his blood.

Ask:

● **Is there enough evidence for you to believe this theory? If so, explain.** (Answers will vary.)

Have the agent for the vision theory share his or her group's theory and conclusions.

Ask:

● **If it was just a hallucination, why don't those who support this theory show us Jesus' body?** (They can't find it; it's long gone; because Jesus came back to life.)

● **Almost every one of Jesus' followers who claimed to have seen Jesus alive was later tortured and killed for his beliefs. If they made up this story, why were so many willing to die for what they'd said?** (They were crazy; they were telling the truth; they'd told the story so long they all believed it.)

● **Is there enough evidence for you to believe this theory? If so, explain.** (Answers will vary.)

Have the agent for the deceptive disciples theory share.

Ask:

● **How did these disciples, who hid during the Crucifixion, suddenly have the courage to sneak past the Roman guards?** (They gathered together for a pep talk; they were still afraid and in hiding.)

● **How could the guards fall so soundly asleep that they couldn't hear the stone being rolled away?** (It had been a long day; they were on drugs.)

● **Why would the guards be so careless when they knew they could be executed if the body was stolen?** (They weren't paying attention; there really was an angel, and they passed out from fear.)

Say: **Again, there's the question of why the disciples would all stick to their story even though they were tortured and put to death. You'd think at least _one_ of them would've changed his story if it were all a lie!**

Ask:

● **Is there enough evidence for you to believe this theory? If so, explain.** (Answers will vary.)

Have the agent for the risen Savior theory share.

Ask:

● **What problems do you have believing this theory?** (A person simply can't come back to life; I don't have a problem with it.)

● **What are reasons for believing this theory?** (God is powerful enough to do anything; there are no contradictions among the accounts of Matthew, Mark, Luke, and John; it follows the prophecies about Jesus' death; it follows what Jesus said would happen.)

● **After considering the evidence for these various theories, what do you think about the**

Teacher Tip

Be prepared to answer students who may have further questions. Be sure not to put them down, but encourage them to continue thinking about the evidence with an open mind. You may want to arrange to meet with these students later for deeper discussion.

claim that Jesus rose from the dead? (I'm more confident in my belief; I feel stronger in my faith; like a lot of my questions have been answered.)

Say: **We can have intelligent and confident faith in the Resurrection, because the evidence and facts support it. And, with the guidance of the Holy Spirit, we can learn to trust and accept Jesus' sacrifice for our sins.**

COMMITMENT
(5 to 10 minutes)

VICTORY PENNANTS

Read 1 Corinthians 15:1-8, 55-58.

Say: **Because Jesus was victorious over death, we have the opportunity to be victorious over sin. If we place our faith in Jesus and establish a relationship with him, we'll be victorious over death and live forever.**

Have kids make pennants out of construction paper with the words "Victory in Jesus" written across one side. Have kids help each other tape their pennants to their own backs.

Have students move about the room and write brief notes on others' pennants, encouraging them to live victoriously for Jesus. For example, "Be strong because you have victory in Jesus!" or "Keep doing what's right because Jesus gives us victory!"

Have students write as many notes as time allows.

Say: **Keep these pennants as reminders of Jesus' power over death. His power can give us victory over sin every day.**

CLOSING
(up to 5 minutes)

☐ OPTION 1: MUSICAL EASTER BASKET

Cut 3×5 cards in half and on them write a topic kids can share with the rest of the class, such as "Tell about your favorite Easter," "Name something you'll do differently this Easter to remember Jesus," or "Tell about a time God helped you be victorious."

Put the cards face down in an Easter basket and have students stand in a circle. Play music on a tape player while kids pass the basket. Randomly stop the music and have the person holding the basket pull out a card and do what it says.

(If your class is large, make two baskets and have two groups going at the same time. Use the same stops of the tape recorder for both groups.)

Continue playing as time allows, then close with prayer, thanking God for giving students victory through Jesus and asking God to help kids express this victory over sin to others.

☐ OPTION 2: BECAUSE HE LIVES

Tear an old bedsheet into large swatches to represent the empty burial cloths of Jesus. Give each student a swatch and a marker. Have kids write on one-half of their swatches, "Because he lives, I have..." completing the sentence with something Christ has added to their lives, such as happiness, eternal life, love, or victory.

On the remaining half of the cloth, have students write, "Because he lives, I will..." and complete that sentence with endings such as "do what's right," "tell others about Jesus," or "have a more thankful attitude."

Encourage kids to keep the cloths someplace that will serve as frequent reminders of this commitment.

Then form a circle and place a large ball (such as a basketball or beach ball) in the circle. Have students take turns "rolling the stone away" by rolling the ball to one another. Have each person catching the ball share in prayer what was on his or her cloth. For example, "Because you live I have eternal life and will tell others about you."

If You Still Have Time ...

Victory Cheer—Form groups of no more than six and have each group create a cheer to celebrate victory in Jesus. Have teams share their cheers with the class, then vote for the team with the best cheer. Close by having everyone do the cheer together.

V-I-C-T-O-R-Y—Give each student a pencil and paper. Have kids write "VICTORY" down the side of their papers and write words or phrases describing the victory God gives over sin. For example, V could be for the **v**ow of eternal life God's given to those who believe in Christ. See if anyone can complete all seven letters.

BODY SEARCH

Photocopy this handout and cut it into four sections. (For larger groups photocopy as needed.)

One way to prove Jesus is not God is to explain why his tomb was empty. If Christ is not risen, then where was his body?

The Swoon Theory

This theory suggests that Christ did not actually die on the cross, but only "swooned" or fainted. Thinking he was dead, the soldiers placed Jesus in the tomb, and when he revived he left the tomb and appeared to his followers.

One way to prove Jesus is not God is to explain why his tomb was empty. If Christ is not risen, then where was his body?

The Vision Theory

This theory suggests that Jesus' followers believed he had come back to life because  they were hallucinating. The disciples so badly wanted Jesus to be alive that they lost touch with reality and were actually seeing things that weren't there.

One way to prove Jesus is not God is to explain why his tomb was empty. If Christ is not risen, then where was his body?

The Deceptive Disciples Theory

This theory claims the disciples stole Jesus' body and lied when they said he'd risen.

 One way to prove Jesus is not God is to explain why his tomb was empty. If Christ is not risen, then where was his body?

The Risen Savior Theory

This theory claims Jesus did indeed die and come to life again three days later just as he'd promised. Jesus had the power to do this because he was the Son of God.

LET THE CELEBRATION BEGIN, AND CONTINUE

The world today offers young people false hope in the midst of chaos and sin. Power, prestige, popularity, and materialism are just a few of the dead-end streets teenagers are encouraged to travel in their search for security. Help your students rely on the true hope they have in Jesus, not just during the Easter season, but 365 days a year.

To help students recognize and celebrate the hope of eternal life we have because of the Resurrection.

LESSON AIM

Students will:
● compare their spiritual lives to seeds,
● discover the source of new spiritual life and its results, and
● determine ways to celebrate the hope Easter brings all year long.

OBJECTIVES

Look up the following verses. Then read the background paragraphs to see how the passages relate to your junior highers and middle schoolers.

1 Corinthians 15:17-22, 42-44 explains the importance of the Resurrection.

BIBLE BASIS
1 CORINTHIANS 15:17-22, 42-44

If Christ didn't rise from the dead, there would be no forgiveness of sin. And just as we're all affected by Adam's sin, we all have the opportunity for forgiveness and new life through Christ. Because of Christ, our worthless bodies will one day be raised in glory.

This passage can help students see why Christians place so much importance on the Resurrection and Easter. If Christ is powerless over sin, so are they. These verses also offer hope, as they describe the changes we'll undergo when we reach heaven.

THIS LESSON AT A GLANCE

Section	Minutes	What Students Will Do	Supplies
Opener (Option 1)	5 to 10	**A Drop in the Bucket**—Contrast eternity to life on earth.	Two buckets for each team, water, small containers
(Option 2)		**A Window Into Heaven**—Imagine what heaven is like.	Newsprint, markers, tape, Bibles
Action and Reflection	15 to 20	**Seeds of New Life**—Compare seeds and grown plants to spiritual life.	Potting soil, spoons, pitcher, water, seeds, cups
Bible Application	10 to 15	**New Light and Life**—Understand how new and eternal life is available to us.	Bible, flashlight
Commitment	5 to 10	**Shine On**—Share ways Christ shines through others.	Flashlight
Closing (Option 1)	up to 5	**Celebration Calendar**—Plan ways to celebrate Easter each month of the year.	
(Option 2)		**Hope Chest**—Share and pray for hopes for the future.	Cardboard box

The Lesson

OPENER
(5 to 10 minutes)

☐ OPTION 1: A DROP IN THE BUCKET

Form teams of no more than four and line up single file at one end of the room for a relay race.

Place a bucket full of water at the front of each team's line and an empty bucket across from its line at the other end of the room. Give each team a tiny container such as an eye-dropper, thimble, or the lid to a small container. Have teams race to see which can be first to fill up its empty bucket by transferring water from the full bucket using the little containers. After a few minutes, call time and congratulate the team transferring the most water.

Say:

● **Describe your feelings about this game.** (I felt surprised at how little water we were able to move; frustrated that we didn't get larger containers for such a huge amount of water.)

● **How does the amount of water you can hold in your container compare to how much water the bucket can hold?** (There's a huge difference; it would take forever to move all that water with this tiny thing.)

● **How's this like the comparison between the time we'll spend on earth and the time in all eternity?** (Eternity is much greater; it makes life seem short by comparison.)

Say: **Whenever you feel like a day is dragging, consider this. If the water in your bucket were eternity, the whole history of mankind would fit into one drop. Our life on earth is just the beginning of a long relationship with God. Because of Christ's victory over death, we can look forward to spending all of eternity with Christ in heaven, and that's a long, long time!**

☐ OPTION 2: A WINDOW INTO HEAVEN

Draw a window frame around the edges of a large sheet of newsprint and title it "A Window Into Heaven." Tape it to a wall.

As students arrive, give them markers and have them draw pictures or write a few words on the window to illustrate what they believe heaven will be like.

Ask:

● **As you were deciding what to draw or write, what kind of feelings did you have about heaven?** (Unsure about what to expect there; hopeful; anxious.)

Have one student read Revelation 21:1-4 and another read Revelation 22:3-5.

Ask:

● **How do these verses make you feel about heaven?** (Like it's a great place; like I'd be happy there.)

Say: **The Bible describes heaven as a more wonderful place than human words can adequately express. In this lesson, we're going to learn more about what Christians have to look forward to each day and for eternity and how Jesus made it all possible.**

SEEDS OF NEW LIFE

On a table place a bag of potting soil, several large spoons, a pitcher of water, and packets of various types of seeds. Give each student a plastic cup.

Have kids put a couple spoonfuls of soil in their cups,

newsprint

ACTION AND REFLECTION
(15 to 20 minutes)

plant a few seeds, then cover them with another spoonful of soil. They can then add a little water.

When everyone has planted their seeds, have students pick up their cups and carry them outdoors. Look at the surrounding trees, flowers, grass, and other growing plants. Have kids celebrate the growing trees and plants by cheering and applauding for at least one minute.

Ask:

● **What are your thoughts about your seed as you compare it to everything growing around us?** (It's so small by comparison; it's strange to think a tree could grow from a seed; it seems like it'll be a long time before my seed ever looks like anything; I don't think my seed will ever be as big as these things around us.)

● **How are the seeds we planted like our spiritual lives?** (They can grow into something beautiful if we care for them; there's not much to see at the beginning, but God changes us and makes us grow.)

● **How are the seeds different from our spiritual lives?** (These plants will die someday, but our life with God is eternal; sometimes it's easier to see growth in a plant than in our lives.)

● **Just as the plants around us are at various stages of growth, we're all at different stages of spiritual growth. Can you think of someone who's like a spiritual tree, showing spiritual strength and growth?** (Answers will vary.)

● **Your seed was once part of another plant. Even if the old plant dies, it leaves a seed to create new life. How is this like the new life God plants in us?** (Our old ways die, and God's new ways grow; Christ had to die so we could have new life.)

● **How is the taste of a celebration we had through our cheers like the taste of heaven we get as followers of Christ?** (Heaven will be a party; we can be joyful today as we think about heaven.)

Say: **If Jesus hadn't come back to life we'd have no new life. Let's return to our room and see how the Bible explains this.**

Return to your classroom.

TEACHER TIP

If your church has an appropriate area available, do this activity in a garden spot, planting seeds that will grow into a new bed of flowers.

BIBLE APPLICATION
(10 to 15 minutes)

NEW LIGHT AND LIFE

Read the following verses aloud, using the room's lights to help kids understand the contrast Paul is describing. (The reader will need a flashlight. You may want to have a helper operate the light switch as you read. If so, agree on a signal so the switch operator will know when to turn the lights off and on.)

1 Corinthians 15:17-22, 42-44

And if Christ has not been raised (lights off), **then your**

faith has nothing to it; you are still guilty of your sins. And those in Christ who have already died are lost. If our hope in Christ is for this life only, we should be pitied more than anyone else in the world. But Christ has truly been raised from the dead (lights on)—the first one and proof that those who sleep in death will also be raised. Death (lights off) has come because of what one man did, but the rising (lights on) from death also comes because of one man. In Adam all of us die (lights out). In the same way, in Christ all of us will be made alive again (lights on).

It is the same with the dead who are raised to life. The body that is "planted" will ruin and decay (lights off), but it is raised to a life that cannot be destroyed (lights on). When the body is "planted," it is without honor (lights off), but it is raised in glory (lights on). When the body is "planted," it is weak (lights off), but when it is raised, it is powerful (lights on). The body that is "planted" is a physical body (lights off). When it is raised, it is a spiritual body (lights on).

Form pairs and have partners take turns answering the following questions:

● **What was the significance of the light effects?** (The light represented Jesus; the light was life; the dark represented sin; darkness was death.)

● **What do these verses mean to you?** (We can't have new life without Jesus; God can change us from something dead and ugly to something alive and beautiful.)

● **What is the "seed" or starting point for a new spiritual life?** (Believing Jesus died and came back to life; believing Jesus is God.)

● **Have you "planted" this seed in your life?** (Answers will vary. This may be a good time to extend an invitation to follow Jesus.)

● **How would your life be different if Jesus hadn't risen from the dead?** (I wouldn't know how to be forgiven for the wrong things I do; I'd have no hope of heaven; I wouldn't have a relationship with God.)

Say: **It's through the life, death, and resurrection of Jesus that we have hope of eternal life. This life begins here and extends to the heavenly home we'll see some- day. That's what we should celebrate at Easter.**

SHINE ON

Say: **Even though Easter comes only once a year, we can celebrate new life through Christ's resurrection every day by shining the light of Jesus on those around us.**

Turn off the room lights and shine the flashlight on a student. Tell this person one way you've seen the light of Jesus shine in his or her life. For example, "I've seen Jesus shine through your positive attitude," or "I've seen Jesus shine through your willingness to help others." Hand the light

COMMITMENT
(5 to 10 minutes)

to the person and have him or her shine it on another student, sharing as you did. Continue until all students have had the light shined on them and everyone has shined the light on someone else.

Say: **Let's remember to shine our lights all year, reminding others of our new life in Christ each day.**

CLOSING
(up to 5 minutes)

☐ OPTION 1: CELEBRATION CALENDAR

Form six groups. (A group can be one person.) Assign each group two months of the year. (If your group is large enough, form twelve groups and assign each group only one month.)

Have each group share at least one way to celebrate the true meaning of Easter during each of its months. These ideas can be related to other holidays or entirely new celebrations.

Close with one-word prayers. Have each person say only one word to represent his or her thanks to God for Easter, such as "life," "hope," "heaven," or simply "thanks."

☐ OPTION 2: HOPE CHEST

Place a large cardboard box in the center of the room.

Say: **This represents our class "hope chest." It stands for our hopes for the future. And as we've learned, the future holds a lot of time!**

Have students take turns standing in the hope chest and sharing something they hope to see happen in the coming year. Close by asking God to turn these hopes into reality.

If You Still Have Time . . .

Heaven on Earth—Have kids brainstorm what heaven might be like. A party every day? Disneyland? No school? Discuss how knowing we can go to heaven makes life on earth better. How does this knowledge make our lives different?

Course Reflection—Form a circle. Ask students to reflect on the past four lessons. Have them take turns completing the following sentences:
- Something I learned in this course is . . .
- If I could tell my friends about this course, I'd say . . .
- Something I'll do differently because of this course is . . .

BONUS IDEAS

Bonus Scriptures—The lessons focus on a select few scripture passages, but if you'd like to incorporate more Bible readings into the lessons, here are some suggestions:
- Isaiah 53:3-12 (Jesus' suffering is foretold.)
- Matthew 27:32-66 (Matthew tells of Jesus' death and burial.)
- Mark 8:31-33 (Jesus predicts his death and resurrection.)
- Acts 10:38-43 (Peter shares his faith with Cornelius.)
- Romans 3:22-26 (Belief in Christ brings forgiveness.)
- Galatians 3:13-14 (Christ took our place.)

Sunrise Service—Have students plan and lead an Easter sunrise service for your church. (If your church already has such a service, see if students can be involved in it.) Allow them to be creative in planning songs and drama and sharing the true meaning of Easter.

Bringing Up Baby—Have kids bring baby pictures of themselves (you may have to ask parents to help!). Display the pictures around the room and have students see if they can identify one another. Reveal the identity of each picture and see who had the most correct guesses.

Discuss the changes that occur during years of physical growth and what's necessary for these changes to happen. Compare this growth to spiritual growth and the things necessary for it to occur.

Egg Hunt—Have students organize an Easter egg hunt for children near your church's neighborhood. Have students write on slips of paper various verses they feel express parts of the Easter message. Include these in plastic eggs along with a few pieces of candy. Before the hunt, have several students briefly share the true message of Easter with the kids.

Eastre Becomes Easter—Share with students the origins of Easter:

Thousands of years ago people in Northern Europe celebrated a festival called Eastre. This was the name of their goddess of spring, and the holiday was a time to celebrate new life in nature at winter's end.

When Jesus Christ rose from the dead, this spring festival took on new meaning. Instead of celebrating new life in nature, Christ's followers celebrated the new

---

MEETINGS AND MORE

spiritual life they'd found through him. Old festival customs continued but were given new Christian meanings. Eastre became Easter.

Hold up the items listed below (or pictures of them) and see if students can guess the original meanings these items had during Eastre. Then have kids see if they can think of new Christian meanings for them.

● New clothes (originally represented the clean, new spring season).

● Eggs (originally represented new life).

● Rabbits (originally represented fertility and new life).

Jewish Seder—Invite a representative from Jews for Jesus to provide a traditional Jewish Seder for your group. Or do some research and plan this event yourself. Explain to the kids the meaning, symbolism, and history behind the various elements of the Passover meal. (Check your church library for resources to help you.)

Heavenly Scavenger Hunt—Send kids on a scavenger hunt for articles that somehow illustrate what eternity with God will be like. Encourage kids to be creative. (They can use Revelation 21-22 for ideas.) For example, a handkerchief may remind them that in heaven there will be no more crying. Set a time limit and have kids regroup and share how each of their items represents eternity with God.

Sunday's on the Way—Obtain a tape of Carman's song, "Sunday's on the Way," and play it for the class. Have kids discuss their feelings as they listened to the song.

Check Your Vital Signs—Give each student a copy of the "Signs of Life" handout (p. 46) to complete. (Don't ask students to share their responses aloud.)

Discuss how each sign of life is demonstrated by plants and animals and how it can be shown in a Christian's life. Then have students share their answers to the last question.

Have students form groups of four and pray together. Have one person in each group pray for the others in the group to show renewed life by *growing* in Christ. Have the next person pray for renewed life in the group by *regeneration* and winning others to Jesus. Have the third person pray for the group to *consume* God's Word, and have the last person pray for the group to be more *sensitive.*

Table Talk—Give students the opportunity to prepare and serve an Easter dessert to their parents. After eating, have parents share special Easter memories. Allow time for students to share how Christ's resurrection has changed their lives.

Have parents and students work together to complete the "Table Talk" handout (p. 19) during this event.

Easter Eggstravaganza—Since eggs are commonly associated with Easter, and many forms of life originate with eggs, throw an Easter Eggstravaganza. Serve egg rolls, egg salad, egg foo yong, nonalcoholic eggnog, and other foods using eggs as a main ingredient.

Have an egg toss, egg decorating contest, and egg hunt. Decide which came first: the chicken or the egg. See who can tell the worst egg "yoke" (joke).

Finally, be sure everyone knows why eggs don't tell the real Easter story. They're necessary for physical life to begin, but they aren't necessary for new spiritual life to begin. Jesus Christ gives us new eternal life through belief in him.

New Life—Plan a retreat around the theme of new life. Use scripture passages to help students understand how Jesus' death and resurrection give us the chance to have a new spiritual life. Use the "new" theme throughout the retreat, playing new games and learning new songs. Include games where students create a new animal or machine, and have a contest to see which team can create a new food out of various foods provided.

Plan sessions on topics such as
● How do I get new life?
● How does this new life grow?
● What will hinder this growth?
● What are the rewards of new life?

PARTY PLEASER

RETREAT IDEA

SIGNS OF LIFE

Jesus died and rose again to give us new life in him. Complete this handout to help you determine how much vitality your spiritual life shows. Make a mark on the line under each statement to indicate your vital signs.

Living things grow. Are you growing in your relationship with Christ, or is your spiritual life stuck in neutral?

_____

no growth   vital growth

Living things generate new life. Are you doing all you can to help other people know Jesus, or are you keeping this good news to yourself?

_____

not sharing your faith   sharing your faith often

Living things consume other things which become a part of them. Are you feeding on God's Word daily and making it a part of yourself, or is your Bible gathering dust somewhere?

_____

not reading at all   reading regularly

Living things are sensitive to their environment. Are you sensitive to the needs and feelings of those around you, or do you think only about your own wants and desires?

_____

not sensitive at all   very sensitive

What can you do to better demonstrate you're alive in Christ?

CURRICULUM REORDER—TOP PRIORITY

Order now to prepare for your upcoming Sunday school classes, youth ministry meetings, and weekend retreats! Each book includes all teacher and student materials—plus photocopiable handouts—for any size class . . . for just $7.99 each!

FOR SENIOR HIGH:

1 & 2 Corinthians: Christian Discipleship, ISBN 1-55945-230-7

Changing the World, ISBN 1-55945-236-6

Christians in a Non-Christian World, ISBN 1-55945-224-2

Christlike Leadership, ISBN 1-55945-231-5

Communicating With Friends, ISBN 1-55945-228-5

Counterfeit Religions, ISBN 1-55945-207-2

Dating Decisions, ISBN 1-55945-215-3

Deciphering Jesus' Parables, ISBN 1-55945-237-4

Exodus: Following God, ISBN 1-55945-226-9

Exploring Ethical Issues, ISBN 1-55945-225-0

Faith for Tough Times, ISBN 1-55945-216-1

Forgiveness, ISBN 1-55945-223-4

Getting Along With Parents, ISBN 1-55945-202-1

Getting Along With Your Family, ISBN 1-55945-233-1

The Gospel of John: Jesus' Teachings, ISBN 1-55945-208-0

Hazardous to Your Health: AIDS, Steroids & Eating Disorders, ISBN 1-55945-200-5

Is Marriage in Your Future?, ISBN 1-55945-203-X

Jesus' Death & Resurrection, ISBN 1-55945-211-0

The Joy of Serving, ISBN 1-55945-210-2

Knowing God's Will, ISBN 1-55945-205-6

Life After High School, ISBN 1-55945-220-X

Making Good Decisions, ISBN 1-55945-209-9

Money: A Christian Perspective, ISBN 1-55945-212-9

Movies, Music, TV & Me, ISBN 1-55945-213-7

Overcoming Insecurities, ISBN 1-55945-221-8

Responding to Injustice, ISBN 1-55945-214-5

Revelation, ISBN 1-55945-229-3

School Struggles, ISBN 1-55945-201-3

Sex: A Christian Perspective, ISBN 1-55945-206-4

Today's Lessons From Yesterday's Prophets, ISBN 1-55945-227-7

Turning Depression Upside Down, ISBN 1-55945-135-1

What Is the Church?, ISBN 1-55945-222-6

Who Is God?, ISBN 1-55945-218-8

Who Is Jesus?, ISBN 1-55945-219-6

Who Is the Holy Spirit?, ISBN 1-55945-217-X

Your Life as a Disciple, ISBN 1-55945-204-8

FOR JUNIOR HIGH/MIDDLE SCHOOL:

Accepting Others: Beyond Barriers & Stereotypes, ISBN 1-55945-126-2

Advice to Young Christians: Exploring Paul's Letters, ISBN 1-55945-146-7

Applying the Bible to Life, ISBN 1-55945-116-5

Becoming Responsible, ISBN 1-55945-109-2

Bible Heroes: Joseph, Esther, Mary & Peter, ISBN 1-55945-137-8

Boosting Self-Esteem, ISBN 1-55945-100-9

Building Better Friendships, ISBN 1-55945-138-6

Can Christians Have Fun?, ISBN 1-55945-134-3

Caring for God's Creation, ISBN 1-55945-121-1

Christmas: A Fresh Look, ISBN 1-55945-124-6

Competition, ISBN 1-55945-133-5

Dealing With Death, ISBN 1-55945-112-2

Dealing With Disappointment, ISBN 1-55945-139-4

Drugs & Drinking, ISBN 1-55945-118-1

Evil and the Occult, ISBN 1-55945-102-5

Genesis: The Beginnings, ISBN 1-55945-111-4

Guys & Girls: Understanding Each Other, ISBN 1-55945-110-6

Handling Conflict, ISBN 1-55945-125-4

Heaven & Hell, ISBN 1-55945-131-9

Is God Unfair?, ISBN 1-55945-108-4

Love or Infatuation?, ISBN 1-55945-128-9

Making Parents Proud, ISBN 1-55945-107-6

Making the Most of School, ISBN 1-55945-113-0

Materialism, ISBN 1-55945-130-0

Miracles!, ISBN 1-55945-117-3

Peace & War, ISBN 1-55945-123-8

Peer Pressure, ISBN 1-55945-103-3

Prayer, ISBN 1-55945-104-1

Reaching Out to a Hurting World, ISBN 1-55945-140-8

Sermon on the Mount, ISBN 1-55945-129-7

Suicide: The Silent Epidemic, ISBN 1-55945-145-9

Telling Your Friends About Christ, ISBN 1-55945-114-9

The Ten Commandments, ISBN 1-55945-127-0

Today's Music: Good or Bad?, ISBN 1-55945-101-7

What Is God's Purpose for Me?, ISBN 1-55945-132-7

What's a Christian?, ISBN 1-55945-105-X

Order today from your local Christian bookstore, or write: Group Publishing, Box 485, Loveland, CO 80539. For mail orders, please add postage/handling of $4 for orders up to $15, $5 for orders of $15.01+. Colorado residents add 3% sales tax.

BRING THE BIBLE TO LIFE FOR YOUR 5TH- AND 6TH-GRADERS WITH GROUP'S *HANDS-ON BIBLE CURRICULUM*™

Energize your kids with Active Learning!

Group's **Hands-On Bible Curriculum**™ will help you teach the Bible in a radical new way. It's based on Active Learning—the same teaching method Jesus used.

Research shows that we retain less than 10% of what we hear or read. *But we remember up to 90% of what we experience.* Your 5th- and 6th-graders will experience spiritual lessons and learn to apply them to their daily lives! And—they'll go home remembering what they've learned.

In each lesson, students will participate in exciting and memorable learning experiences using fascinating gadgets and gizmos you've not seen with any other curriculum. Your 5th- and 6th-graders will discover biblical truths and <u>remember</u> what they learn—because they're <u>doing</u> instead of just listening.

You'll save time and money too!

While students are learning more, you'll be working less—simply follow the quick and easy instructions in the **Teachers Guide**. You'll get tons of material for an energy-packed 35- to 60-minute lesson. And, if you have extra time, there's an arsenal of Bonus Ideas and Time Stuffers to keep kids occupied—and learning! Plus, you'll SAVE BIG over other curriculum programs that require you to buy expensive separate student books—all student handouts in Group's **Hands-On Bible Curriculum**™ are photocopiable!

In addition to the easy-to-use **Teachers Guide**, you'll get all the essential teaching materials you need in a ready-to-use **Learning Lab**™. No more running from store to store hunting for lesson materials—all the active-learning tools you need to teach 13 exciting Bible lessons to any size class are provided for you in the **Learning Lab**™.

Challenging topics every 13 weeks keep your kids coming back!

Group's **Hands-On Bible Curriculum**™ covers topics that matter to your kids and teaches them the Bible with integrity. Every quarter you'll explore three meaningful subjects. One is centered around learning about <u>others</u> . . . another helps your students learn about <u>themselves</u> . . . and a third teaches your kids about <u>God</u>. Switching topics every month keeps your 5th- and 6th-graders enthused and coming back for more. The full 2-year program will help your kids . . .

● make God-pleasing decisions,
● recognize their God-given potential, and
● seek to grow as Christians.

Take the boredom out of Sunday school, children's church, and youth group for your 5th- and 6th-graders. Make your job easier and more rewarding with no-fail lessons that are ready in a flash. Order Group's **Hands-On Bible Curriculum**™ for your 5th- and 6th-graders today.

QUARTER 1, YEAR B
Teachers Guide	**ISBN 1-55945-314-1**	**$14.99**
Learning Lab™	**ISBN 1-55945-315-X**	**$34.99**

QUARTER 2, YEAR B
Teachers Guide	**ISBN 1-55945-316-8**	**$14.99**
Learning Lab™	**ISBN 1-55945-317-6**	**$34.99**

Order today from your local Christian bookstore, or write: Group Publishing, Box 485, Loveland, CO 80539. For mail orders, please add postage/handling of $4 for orders up to $15, $5 for orders of $15.01+. Colorado residents add 3% sales tax.